Date: Nov. 10, 2022

To: Jasmine

From: Joyce, Allan and Vince

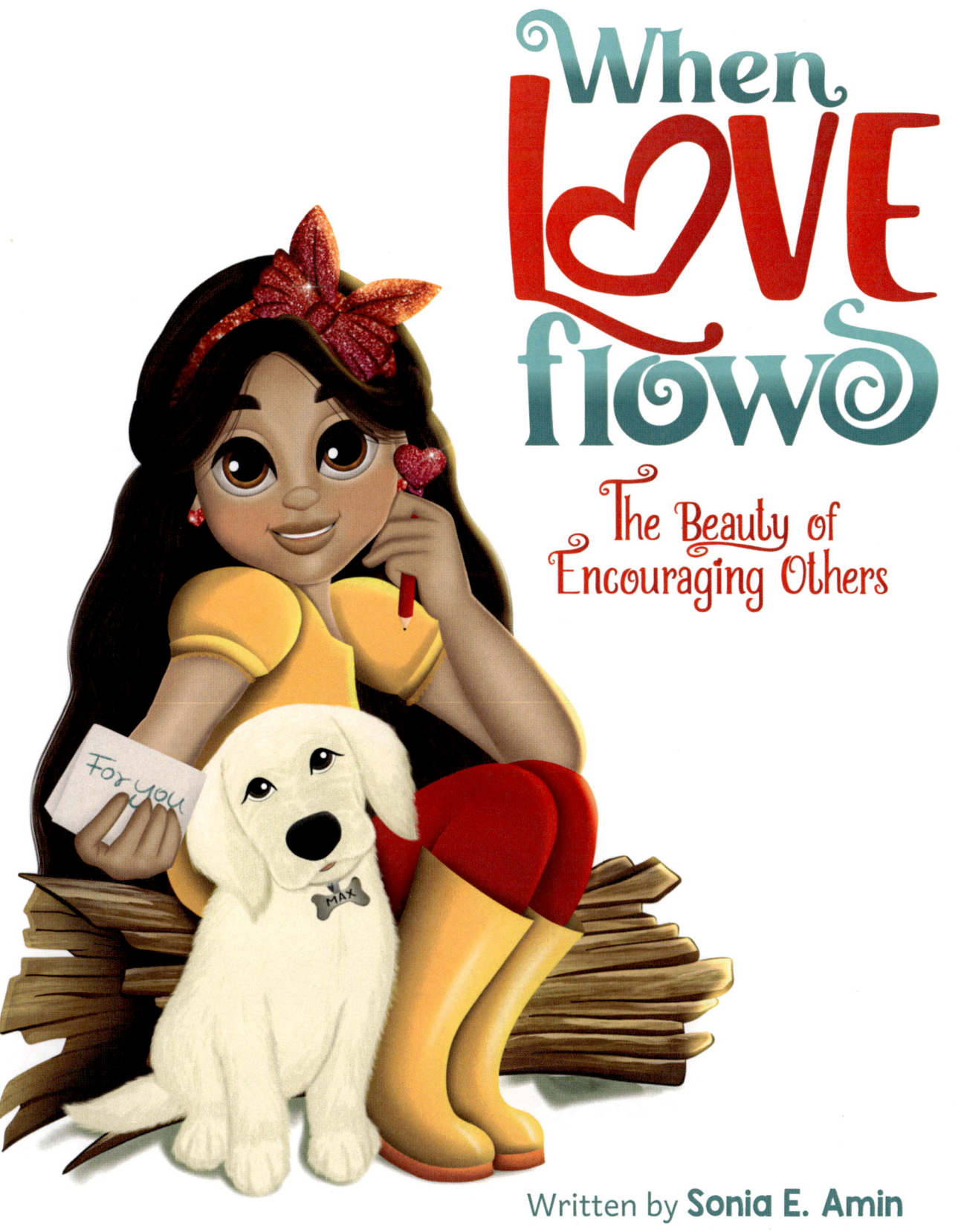

a **flowing** fountain,

a **burbling** brook...

Words were **springing** up in Nora's heart. The kindness, love, and joy in her heart were too much to contain.

She had to share them with the world. She loved the people in her life so much. How could she show them?

Nora grabbed a pen and paper and sat at the kitchen table. The brownies her mom baked the night before were delicious! Nora tried to write the perfect thank-you.

Words **trickled** to a stop.
Nora's words were stuck.

"Time to go to school!"
Nora's mom called.

At school, Ms. Gibbs made class so much fun!

Nora wanted to write the perfect note to thank her teacher.
She picked up her pencil during free time
and gazed down at her paper.

Her thoughts swirled around and around.

Words **trickled** to a stop.
Nora's words were still stuck.

The geyser inside Nora's heart was ready to erupt!

But too many words were trying to **burst** out!

Drip.

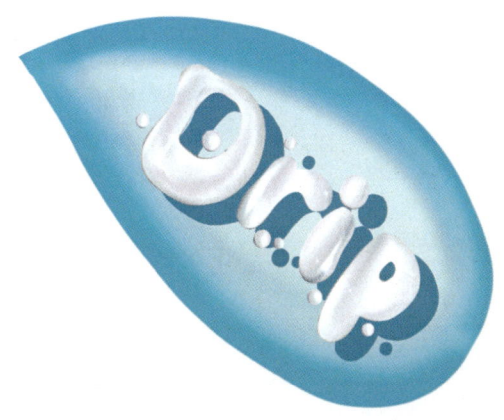

Words **trickled** to a stop.
Nora's words kept getting stuck.

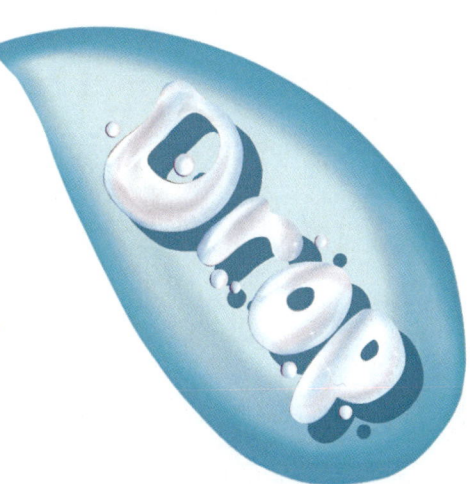

But Nora gave Emma a hand. The words in Nora's heart **poured** out with tenderness.
"I'm here for you, friend."
Emma brushed herself off and grinned.

At home, Nora's sister sighed over her homework assignment.

"This is too hard! I don't understand it."

The words in Nora's heart **poured** out with compassion.

"I'm here for you, Sis."

Nora took a seat nearby, and her sister sat up tall and got to work.

Later that day, Nora's neighbor was sitting on her porch with tears in her eyes.

The love in Nora's heart **stirred.** She raced to the pen and paper she'd left on the kitchen table that morning.

Like a **rippling** river,
a **flowing** fountain,
a **burbling** brook...

The words in Nora's heart
gushed out with love.

With a plate of brownies in hand,
Nora delivered her note.

Ms. Barb gave Nora a big hug,
and the love in Nora's heart **overflowed.**

It **burbles** in the thoughtful acts she does.

It **pours** into the encouraging notes she writes.

Dear Ms. Gibbs,
you are an awesome teacher. Thanks for making class so much fun.
Love,
Nora

Dear mom,
you are the best
I love your hugs and brownies.
Love,
Nora

Ripple, burble, gush.

Her words begin to rush.
The words in Nora's heart flow freely...

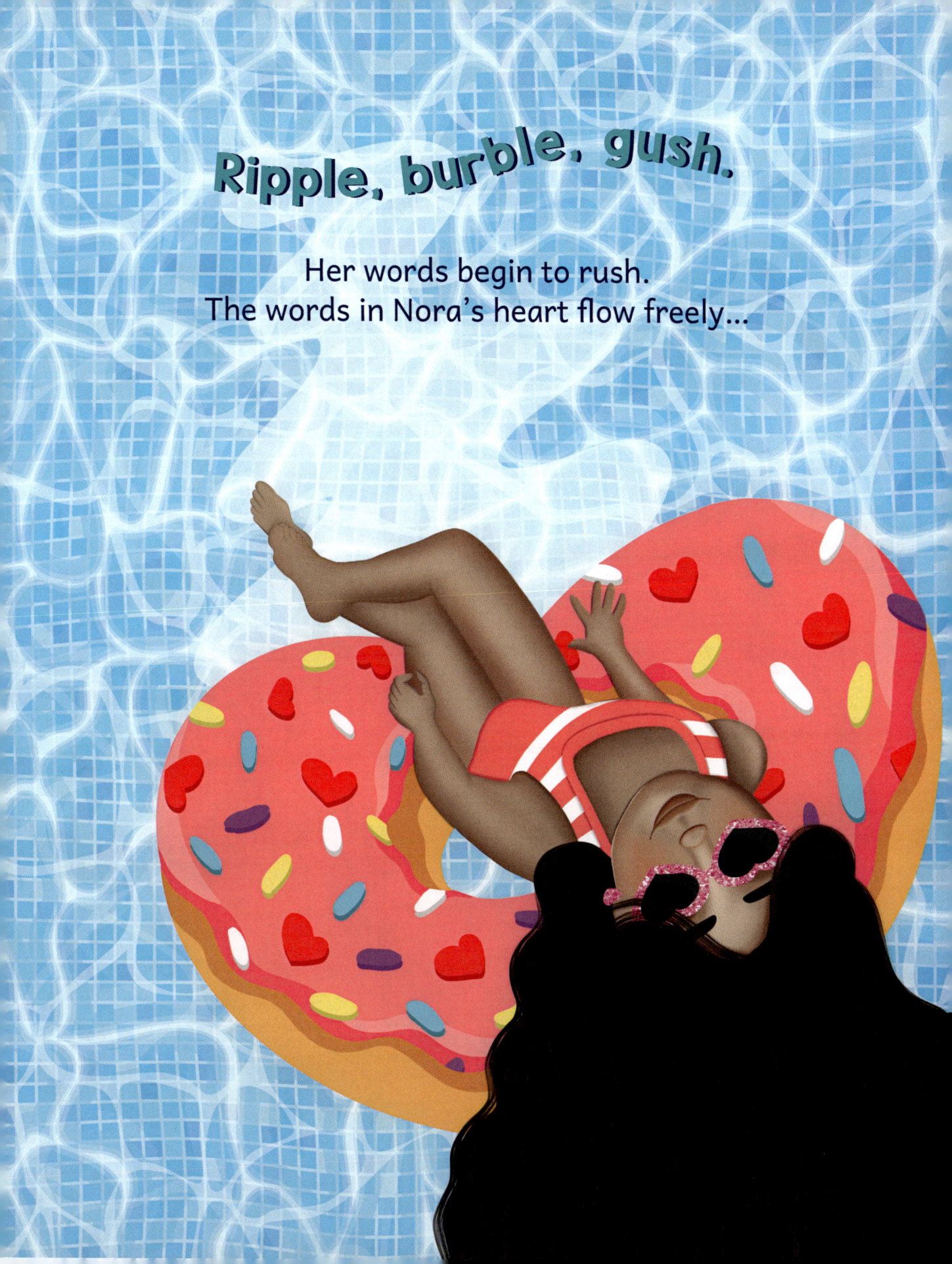

and she shares kindness, love, and joy with the world.

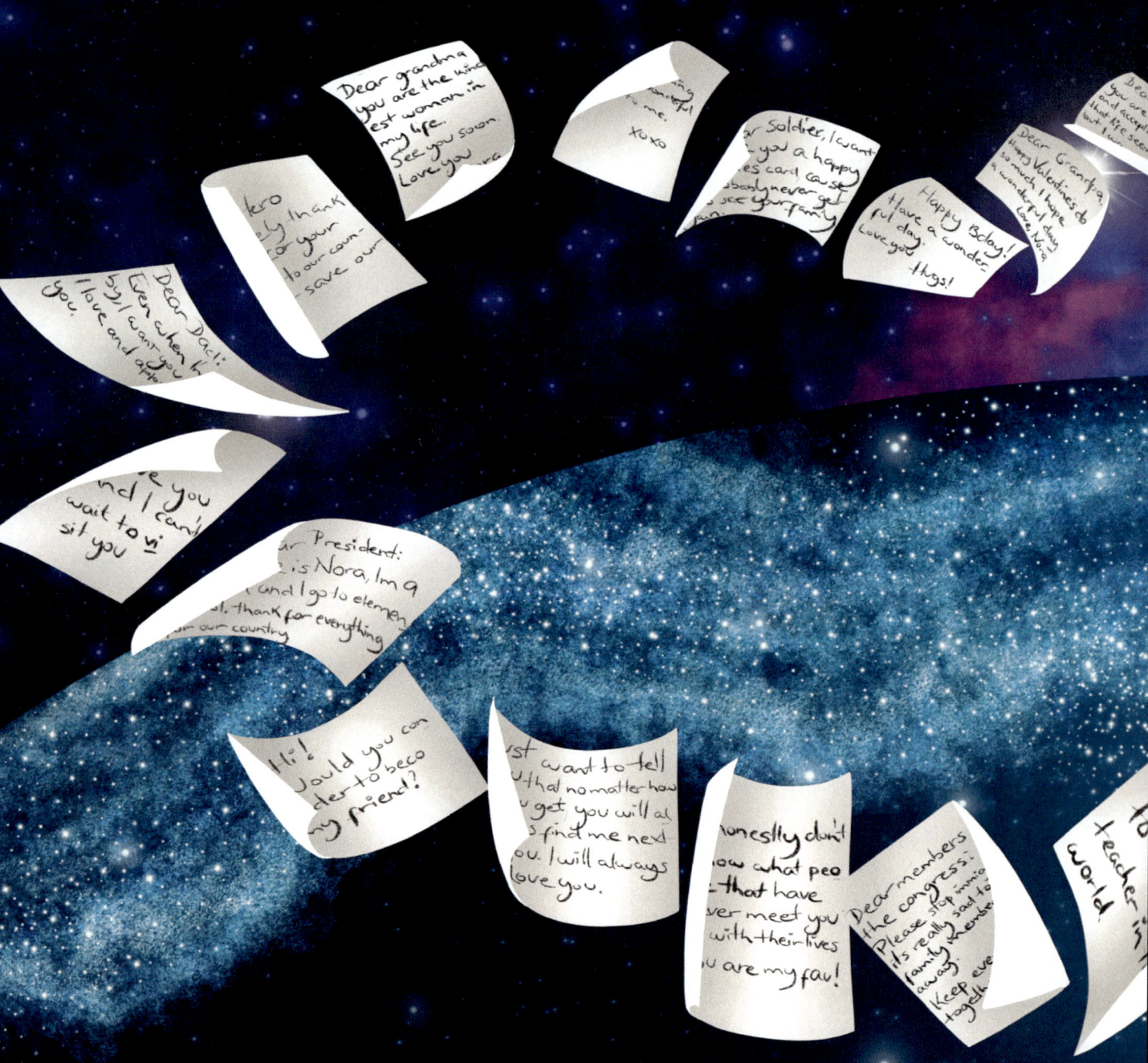

Note to Grown-ups

Encouragement is a simple and priceless gift that can brighten someone's day when they least expect it yet need it most. It can come in many different forms and give hope and strength to those on the receiving end while enriching our own lives.

When Love Flows was inspired by numerous biblical scriptures that impressed on me the mission of loving others wholeheartedly. Nora's story motivates readers to show up as encouragers in their own spheres of influence. By guiding children to know, from a young age, how they can positively impact others, we embolden them to be the world changers they were created to be.

As you read *When Love Flows* with the children in your life, I hope that you and they sense the love poured out from my heart and are inspired to take encouraging action.

May you and yours be encouraged!

Love always,

Sonia

BROWNIE RECIPE

Remember the brownies Nora gave her neighbor?

You can try the recipe yourself!

Point your camera at the QR code and click on the link that pops up!

Glossary

Burble – to make a soft bubbling sound

Compassion – a feeling of wanting to help someone who is sick, hungry, in trouble, or otherwise in need

Encourage – to give help, support, or hope to someone

Erupt – to break or burst out suddenly

Gaze – to look at someone or something in a steady way and usually for a long time

Geyser – a hot spring that sends up fountain-like jets of water from time to time

Gush – to flood out in large amounts and with great force

Muddled – a confused state or mess

Ripple – to form small waves

Trickle – to flow or fall by drops or in a small, gentle stream

Let's Talk About It!

💧 How do you think Nora's neighbor felt after receiving brownies and a thoughtful note from Nora?

💧 Nora was able to pour encouragement into others from the overflow of her heart. Who do you think poured into Nora? (There is no wrong answer.)

💧 What has someone done or said that has encouraged you?

💧 Name a few ways you can encourage your friends and family.

💧 What can you do to show gratitude to someone who has made an impact in your life?

💧 Grab a stack of sticky notes or notecards. Write down simple notes of encouragement you can give to the special people in your life. Don't forget your teachers!

Need help? Here are a few sentence starters:

- Your smile...
- Your friendship is...
- I'm happy to help you with...
- You've got this!
- Thank you for...

Thank You!

Sign up to hear about free downloads and more! Support encouragement in your school by scheduling an author visit or sponsoring copies of *When Love Flows*. Lesson plans are gifted with every booking.

Visit **soniaeamin.com** for more information.

If this book **touched your heart**, please take a moment to leave an honest review on Goodreads or Amazon. This helps other readers discover *When Love Flows* and is one way you can encourage people looking for books like this!

**Check out Sonia's other book,
Bax and His Bubbles!**

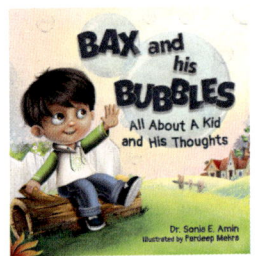

About the Author

Sonia Amin is a pharmacist, speaker, and award-winning author who loves encouraging others with her words, hugs, and prayers. She lives in Florida with her husband and two kids and considers herself a professional snuggler to each of them. She invites you to reach out to her online at soniaeamin.com.

About the Illustrator

Arlenis Chirinos is a Venezuelan illustrator based in Chile. Her baby girl, Sarah, is her greatest inspiration and the driving force behind her work. Arlenis began illustrating to inspire her daughter and future generations with charming and delightful images while reflecting God in her creative work.

Advocating for children around the world is a mission dear to my heart. It's an honor to support the work of charities doing just that through the sales of each book. Some of the organizations my family supports include Mission for Orphans, International Justice Mission, and Compassion International. I encourage you to join me in exploring how you might get involved. —Sonia

To my Savior, Jesus Christ.
May your love always flow through me.
To my precious boys, Asaiah and Malachi.
Mama loves you, forever and always.
—S.A.

To my sweet baby, Sarah. You are my heavenly gift.
—A.C.

Copyright © 2022 by Sonia E. Amin. All rights reserved.

Published in the United States by Sanasamal Press.
www.soniaeamin.com

No part of this book may be reproduced or transmitted in any form or by any means, electronic or mechanical, including photocopying, recording, or by any information storage and retrieval system, without permission in writing from the copyright owner.

Book design by Misty Black Media.

Library of Congress Control Number: 2022907618

Publisher's Cataloging-in-Publication Data
Names: Amin, Sonia E., author. | Chirinos, Arlenis, illustrator.
Title: When love flows : the beauty of encouraging others / by Dr. Sonia E. Amin; illustrated by Arlenis Chirinos.
Description: Debary, FL: Sanasamal Press, 2022. | Summary: Nora shares her love by encouraging people with her kind words, her thoughtful actions, and written notes.
Identifiers: LCCN: 2022907618 | ISBN: 978-1-7352996-7-9 (hardcover) |978-1-7352996-8-6 (paperback) | 978-1-7352996-9-3 (ebook)
Subjects: LCSH Kindness--Juvenile fiction. | Love--Juvenile fiction. | BISAC JUVENILE FICTION / Social Themes / Friendship | JUVENILE FICTION / Social Themes / Values & Virtues | JUVENILE FICTION / Social Themes / General | JUVENILE FICTION / Social Themes / Manners & Etiquette
Classification: LCC PZ7.1.A499 Wh 2022 | DDC [E]--dc23

Made in United States
Orlando, FL
03 November 2022